*Declarations of*

# VICTORY

## Taking a Spiritual Stand Against the Enemy

### CHERYL REGIER

**Declarations of Victory: Taking a Spiritual Stand Against the Enemy**
By Cheryl Regier
Copyright @ 2020 Zachariah House

Published by Zachariah House/Zachariah House Inc.
Website: www.Zachariah-House.com
Email: zachariahhouseofhelps@gmail.com
Facebook: Zachariah House @ZachariahHouseofHelps
Facebook: Cheryl Regier @CherylRegierAuthorEditor

Cover Design & Layout by: ChrisitianAuthorsGetPaid.com
Editor: Kathryn Dakin

All rights reserved. No part of this publication may be reproduced, stored in a retrieval system, or transmitted in any form or by any means—electronic, photocopy, recording, or otherwise—without permission in writing from the author, publisher, or copyright holder, except in the case whereby a reviewer may quote limited passages for review purposes only.

Unless otherwise indicated, all Scripture quotations are from The Passion Translation®. Copyright © 2017, 2018 by Passion & Fire Ministries, Inc. Used by permission. All rights reserved. thePassionTranslation.com.

Scriptures marked NIV are taken from The Holy Bible, New International Version®, NIV® Copyright © 1973, 1978, 1984, 2011 by Biblica, Inc.™ Used by permission. All rights reserved worldwide.

Scriptures marked NKJV are taken from the New King James Version® (NKJV). Copyright © 1982 by Thomas Nelson, Inc. Used by permission. All rights reserved.

DISCLAIMER:
The author designed the information of this book around her own personal experiences along with the truths as found in The Holy Bible. She and the publisher disclaim any liability, loss, or risk incurred by individuals who act on the information presented to them in this book. The author believes the teaching and declarations as presented within to be sound, but readers cannot hold the author, publisher, or any of their agents responsible for either the actions they take or the results of those actions.

Printed in the United States of America

**ISBN: 978-0-9949627-2-0**

# Dedication

To the LORD, my GOD…

It is HE who goes
*with* me to fight *for* me
against my enemies
to give me the victory!

Deuteronomy 20:4

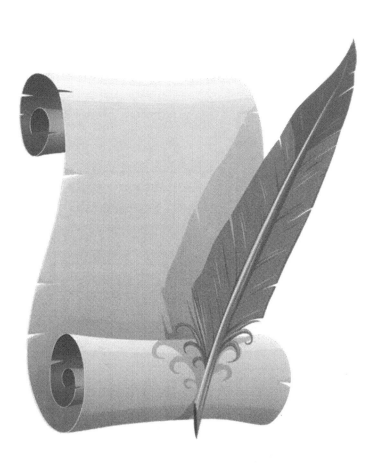

# Acknowledgements

A big THANK YOU to…

The ChristianAuthorsGetPaid.com team
and to my editor, Kathryn Dakin,
for the partnership and ministry
you provided in getting this book
ready for publication.

*Be blessed*

*Blessings!*
*Cheryl*

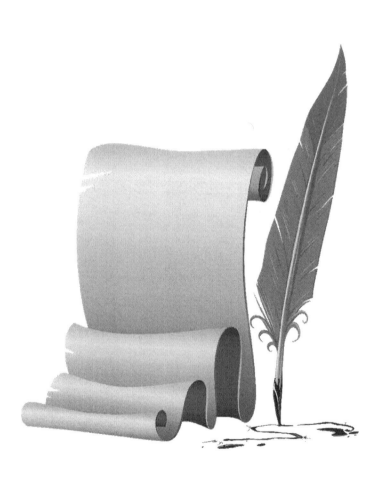

# Foreword

Wow, wow, WOW! The declarations and decrees contained in this powerful little book pack an incredible punch in taking a stand against satan and walking in the wake of the Holy Spirit! I, personally, have used these to position myself in faith and authority for my own life and have seen the strength of God arise within me and His victory manifest.

This book is a much-needed spiritual tool that EVERY believer needs in their toolbelt! It will open up to you a whole new realm of doing battle against the enemy, launching you into living a more fulfilled life according to the purpose for which you have been called as a minister of the Kingdom. Amen? AMEN!

**Kathleen D. Mailer,** #1 Best-Selling Author, International Business Evangelist, Professional Speaker, and Co-founder of Iron Sharpens Iron Ministries. www.KathleenMailer.com;

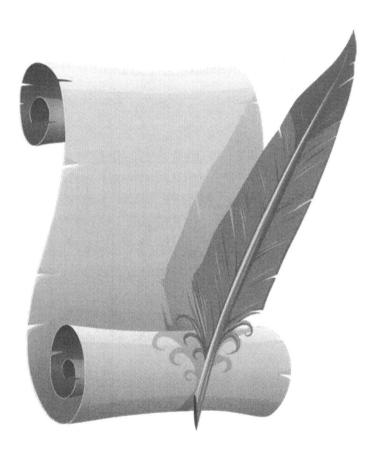

# Table of Contents

| | |
|---|---|
| **Introduction** | 1 |
| **Chapter 1:** <br> What It Means to Declare & Decree | 5 |
| **Chapter 2:** <br> The Word of God | 7 |
| **Chapter 3:** <br> In Faith | 11 |
| **Chapter 4:** <br> The Power of "Yet" | 15 |
| **Chapter 5:** <br> Before You Declare & Decree | 17 |
| **Chapter 6:** <br> Declarations of Victory | 21 |
| **Chapter 7:** <br> Take Your Stand! | 31 |
| **About the Author** | 37 |

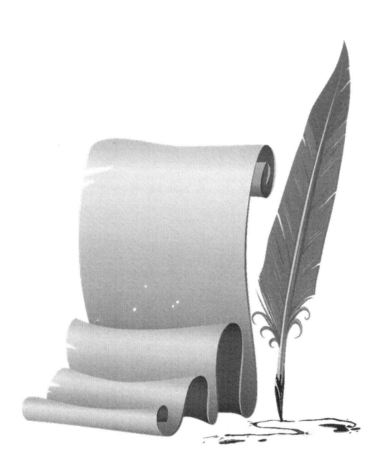

# Introduction

*"Let the words of my mouth
and the meditation of my heart
be acceptable in Your sight,
O Lord, my strength and my Redeemer."*

Psalm 19:14, NKJV

In recent years, the importance of what I am declaring on a daily basis has become more and more apparent. The Lord has been working with me for a while, speaking to me about what is coming out of my mouth and whether or not it lines up with the things of God. However, the lesson of 'declaring and decreeing' has been accelerated and solidified over the last couple of years as I have pursued Him and seen my mind and habits renewed.

In fact, I truly feel like a spiritual shift has taken place, one that has taken the head knowledge of what it means to speak out the victory I have in Jesus to one of knowing and understanding this on a deeper heart and spirit level. As a result, I am finding godly declarations much easier to implement and practice in my life on a daily basis.

Watching what comes out of the mouth is not an easy thing. Ask me how I know! Then, to intentionally decree a thing—in faith believing it to be true for oneself—takes what one is saying to a whole new level. The tongue is a very powerful tool!

This book came about as the result of a specific trial in my life. I was facing a significant 'giant' as an offshoot of another trial my husband and I were dealing with. This giant holds incredible influence in the land, and in my case, was (and is) not one to take on lightly. Thus, I needed to *know* beyond a shadow of a doubt what the Lord had to say on the matter.

The Word is the foundation for each of the decrees found in this book. God brought them to my attention through my personal devotions, or they were impressed upon me at just the right time through other avenues including ministers of the Word, or they were shared with me through my trusted and godly inner circle, again in God's perfect timing. All I can say is that God has been incredibly amazing in His faithfulness to bestow upon me the declarations of victory at the exact time that I needed them to take on the giant I faced.

The declarations set out in this book are specific to when you are facing the strongholds of the enemy and his attacks in your life. As the first book in the "I Declare & Decree" series, it is foundational in its teaching and the fact that, every time you declare and decree the Word of God over your life, you *are* declaring VICTORY! And every time you assert your authority over the devil and his demonic forces, you *are* walking in your mandate and destiny as a child of the living God!

To GOD be the glory, great things He HAS done for me! And I can declare and decree this to be so even now—in my present circumstances—for because of the work on the cross, the victory has already been won for me!

Be encouraged and strengthened as you declare and decree YOUR victory in Jesus' name!

*Cheryl Regier*

Zachariah House Inc.
www.Zachariah-House.com

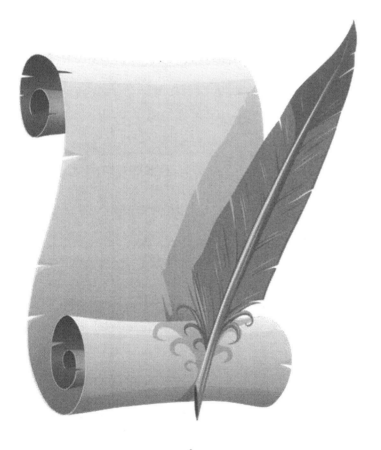

# Chapter One

## What It Means to Declare & Decree

To declare is a highly significant act. The word 'declare' comes from the Latin word *declarare*, which means to 'thoroughly make clear'. Therefore, when we declare something, we are making something completely clear that it is so. We are proclaiming and asserting the truth of a matter in a way that is firm and emphatic.

To decree something carries as much if not more significance then 'to declare'. The word 'decree' is taken from the Latin form of *decretum*, meaning 'something decided'. A decree is defined as 'an official order issued by a legal authority'.[1] In theological terms, a decree refers to 'the eternal purposes of God, by which events are foreordained'.[2]

---

[1] Google dictionary
[2] Dictionary.com

When we declare what God, who is our ultimate authority, has said, we are decreeing His judgment or verdict over that situation or circumstance. We are invoking or putting into legal effect what God says about the matter—His purposes and intentions—and what has already been decided by Him for us, specifically with regard to our future.

In intentionally speaking out what God has given and imparted to us through His Word, we make abundantly clear, both to ourselves and to the principalities and powers of the enemy, that we have the legal and spiritual backing of our Heavenly Father for what we are standing on.

**When we declare and decree, we are exercising our legal right along with the power and authority to receive that which we are believing for.**

## Chapter Two

# The Word of God

I have noticed an interesting shift in my personal devotions. In what can only be described as God's perfect timing, what I have been reading has complemented and confirmed words being brought forward by others in the faith. This has provided exactly what I have needed to personally minister to and share with others and/or has coincided with my current circumstances in life, speaking into them in ways that has both encouraged and equipped me. This shift excites me as I continue to press in and pursue God daily.

The Word of God truly is a living, breathing thing, full of life-giving revelation. It constantly speaks, imparts, teaches, and equips. In facing this one giant as mentioned in my introduction, I went back into my journal to review the Scriptures God had been impressing upon me in my studies. Again, I was amazed at how timely and precise those verses were.

During this same time and from multiple directions, more Scripture came forth that also spoke directly into my situation. Gathering these words—these promises—together, I typed and printed them out so that I could decree them out loud each and every day as my declaration of victory.

Another benefit to my study of the Word has been in reading the Bible from more than one translation in order to get a fuller picture and understanding of God's heart and intention for me. I encourage you to do the same, especially as you prepare your official declarations and decrees.

Now, the WORD of GOD—plus that which He speaks to you and is supported by Scripture—is the legal basis and authority for any declaration and decree that you make. It is by the authority of the Word that a decree is sealed over your life.

> *"So it is impossible for God to lie*
> *for we know that his promise*
> *and his vow will never change!*
> *And now we have run into his heart*
> *to hide ourselves in his faithfulness.*
> *This is where we find*
> *his strength and comfort,*

> ***for he empowers us to seize***
> ***what has already been established***
> ***ahead of time**—an unshakeable hope!"*[3]

Hebrews 6:18

Speaking God's promises <u>out loud</u> is one of the ways we hide ourselves in His faithfulness, arming ourselves with the strength we need to forcibly—in the spirit—seize or take a hold of what has already been established by Him ahead of time. In fact, this verse aligns with another mandate found in The Lord's Prayer where we, as believers, are to be His hands and feet, causing His purposes to be fulfilled on earth just as it is in Heaven.[4]

This is what we are actively doing when we declare and decree—seizing and calling forth into the physical realm that which has already been determined ahead of time by God in the spiritual realm.

And this, my dear friends, is a powerful way to fight our battles!

---

[3] Emphasis mine
[4] See Matthew 6:10

# Chapter Three

## In Faith

Most believers know the Scripture that states that it is impossible to please God without faith.[5] Faith is the activating ingredient to declaring and decreeing the Word over our lives, our situation, and our future. Without it, we are just spouting off mere words.

The good news is that we only need faith as small as a mustard seed[6] to move forward in obedience on our mandate to fulfill God's purposes here on earth as it is in Heaven. What is more exciting than that? When we diligently speak out our declarations as a chosen act of faith in obedience to God, faith *will* grow and increase.

A trust in God and His Word is the very foundation under which our lives as believers is built. A life of faith starts with the choice to believe in what God

---

[5] See Hebrews 11:6
[6] See Matthew 17:20

says and how He sees things. It means that, even in the toughest of situations and despite all the evidence that threatens to drown us in unbelief, the choice is to make God's Word the ultimate authority on the matter. Then, as we act in faith, it *"is all the evidence required to prove what is still unseen."* (Hebrews 11:1) This faith is a powerful and effective tool for operating under our heavenly mandate.

When we are attacked by the enemy, our challenge is to stand in faith. We must choose to believe that God rewards those who passionately seek Him.[7] When we rely on His faithfulness and believe that He will do what He says He will do, we are blessed. However, our eyes must remain on His promises with a heart fixed on that which is far greater. We need to maintain a Kingdom focus.

With this right focus, stepping out to declare and decree the promises of God becomes the answer to overcoming and being victorious in all things.

There is much more that could be said about the importance of faith. Hebrews 11 is a great place to begin learning about the benefits and results of

---

[7] See Hebrews 11:6

living in faith. For now, it is enough to accept that faith is the vehicle that will fuel your declarations, propelling the WORD of God into motion to accomplish God's purposes and intent in your life.

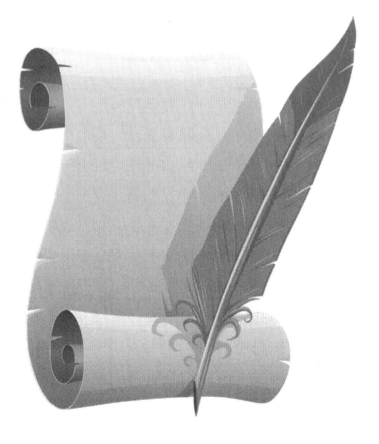

# Chapter Four

## The Power of "Yet"

If God can "*call into being* [declare] *things that don't even exist **yet***",[8] what does that mean for us? Well, there are two sides to every story.

When the enemy is coming at you relentlessly through the circumstances of your life, it is very tempting to spout off in reaction and without thought. Words such as "What next?" or "Why can't I catch a break?" or "Bad things always happen to me," and other such nonsense can come easily to the lips. Unfortunately, this type of response, in all reality, curses you and the situation, declaring into existence things that are <u>not</u> of God.

YET... There is a better way! The power of "yet" aligns our declarations to match God's intentions.

---

[8] Romans 4:17; emphasis mine

*"Though the fig tree does not bud
and there are no grapes on the vines,
though the olive crop fails
and the fields produce no food,
though there are no sheep in the pen
and no cattle in the stalls,
**yet I will** rejoice in the Lord,
I will be joyful in God my Savior."*[9]

Habakkuk 3:17-18, NIV

We were never promised a life without trials and troubles. YET… God has provided a way and a Comforter to bring us the victory. When you respond with "Yet I will…," you prepare the way for greater declarations and decrees of God's Word to go before you in faith and supernatural power.

---

[9] Emphasis mine

# Chapter Five

## Before You Declare & Decree

As you prepare to speak out the declarations of victory in the next chapter, keep the following in mind:

1. **Declare them out loud** – There is incredible power in speaking decrees out loud. Keep in mind that the devil is the prince of the air, so when you speak out loud, you are putting him on official notice and announcing to him what your legal stand is. Furthermore, you build your own faith as you purposefully proclaim God's Word on the matter.

2. **Speak out with confidence** – Say it like you mean it! And mean it! The more you do it, the more confident you will grow in what God intends for you.

3. **Tap into the power of daily confession** – Decrees and declarations, when spoken out

regularly (even daily, especially when facing specific opposition), serve to strengthen and empower you as one serving in the Army of God. The declarations in this book take less than 10 minutes to go through. This is time well spent to receive the equipping you need to take your daily stand against the enemy.

4. **Allow the Holy Spirit to guide your declarations** – I have found that, each time I proclaim these declarations, Holy Spirit has me personalizing them with slight variations. It may be that I expand on a specific decree, add more details about the trial I am currently facing, or the wording of different portions is altered in some way as I boldly speak them out loud. Allow the Holy Spirit to flow as you declare and decree.

5. **Personalize them** – Out of the trial that prompted me to write out these decrees, I added specific details of that trial where fitting and appropriate.

6. **Put the Lord in remembrance** – Each time you utter a decree based on the Word of

God, you are putting God in remembrance of His promises. It says in Isaiah 43:26, *"Put Me in remembrance; Let us contend together; State your case, that you may be acquitted."* (NKJV) In addition, if you have any prophetic words, formal petitions, judgments in your favour received from the Courts of Heaven, dreams or visions that God has given you, or something of this nature that supports your victory in the matter of your specific trial and what you are believing God for, include these things as part of your declarations as you state your case before the Father.

Just like Jesus did during His 40-day temptation in the wilderness,[10] formally and in faith declaring and decreeing the Word serves as your 'statement of defense' against the accusations of the enemy. In speaking out what God says and intends based on His Word, you are allowing that Word to do the work for you. You are letting God defend you and fight your battles.

---

[10] See Matthew 4:1-11

We will have trials in this world,[11] but our Lord has overcome them all! When we live like Jesus, we can do the same. Let THE WORD go forth in power and might on your behalf!

It's time now to declare and decree your victory in Jesus' name!

---

[11] See John 16:33

# Chapter Six

## Declarations of Victory

Because I, _____ *(your name),* have been empowered to seize that which has been established ahead of time in Heaven and by the Word of God, I DECLARE AND DECREE:

I will fight the good fight, which is a fight that I win (and have won) by the power and might of my God working in and through me. I will finish the race, victorious in the name of the Lord and for His glory. I will keep the faith, standing on and speaking out the Word of God and His promises in my life.

~ 2 Timothy 4:7

The Lord stands with me and strengthens me. I am delivered out of the mouth of the lion and his plans against me. Thus, I am delivered from every evil work and have been preserved for His heavenly Kingdom.

~ 2 Timothy 4:17-18

I am not shaken or intimidated by the opposition that has risen up against me, for my courage in the face of the enemy serves as a sure sign of their defeat and of my victory.

~ Philippians 1:28

I will not fear, for my God is always with me. I will not be dismayed or discouraged, for I am the Lord's. He strengthens me and helps me, upholding me with His righteous and victorious right hand.

~ Isaiah 41:10

I do not need to fear, for I will not be ashamed or disgraced. I will not be put to shame, and the shame and disgrace from my past will not be remembered, for it has been repented of, covered by the Blood, forgiven in Jesus' name, and dealt with in the Courts of Heaven.

~ Isaiah 54:4

I am not afraid. Instead, I stand firm, and as a result, I will see the salvation of the Lord, which He will accomplish for me on earth as it is in Heaven. The enemy I see today, I will see and deal with no more, for the Lord fights for me.

~ Exodus 14:13-14

This trial will be brief, for the God of loving grace who imparts all blessing and favour will personally and powerfully restore me and make me stronger than ever. I will be set firmly in place, established and grounded, built up and settled, and positioned for Kingdom work in Jesus' name.

~ 1 Peter 5:10

I fight <u>from</u> victory—the victory is mine in the name of the Lord—for He has already disarmed the powers and principalities of darkness, stripping from them every weapon, including their spiritual authority and power to accuse me.

~ Colossians 2:15

I will succeed in what I choose to do, for the light of God's favour goes before me, guiding my steps and showing me the way. Therefore, I decree this victory over the enemy, and it shall be done and established for me.

~ Job 22:28

As one who has been purchased and purified by the sacrifice of Jesus, I say, "Yes, I am willing to take a stand for what is right and expose sin," and I do so (and have done so) under Holy Spirit direction with the full authority of Heaven behind me as an heir with Christ. I am not and will not be intimidated by the enemy!"

~ Titus 2:15

The One who breaks open, the Messiah, goes before me. Therefore, I am liberated, and a way is made for me to pass through safely in Jesus' name.

~ Micah 2:13

The Lord helps me as my loving Father, coming to my rescue and breaking open the way into a beautiful and broad place. He is <u>for</u> me and on my side, standing beside me as my strong champion.

As a result, I triumph over my enemies and see them defeated.

~ Psalm 118:5-7

What has been meant for evil against me, God is already, even now, turning it around for His glory as well as for my advantage and benefit. I will be strong, for He will avenge me and save me and bring me repayment and blessing.

~ Genesis 50:20, Isaiah 35:4

My God and King raises His voice to command my victory! Through His glorious name and awesome power, I push through to that victory, defeating every enemy coming against me, for I trust not my own strength and the weapons and strategies of the world but rely on my Lord and Savior for deliverance.

~ Psalm 44:4-7

As I prepare to meet my enemy, the Lord's superabundant grace is already powerfully working in me, releasing within me all forms of spiritual wisdom and practical understanding so that when (or if) I face my accuser, I will do so with complete confidence, allowing the Spirit of Wisdom—that which is pure and Holy Spirit-inspired—to reveal to me, even in the moment, what I am to say.

~ Ephesians 1:8, Luke 12:12

God gives life, so even against all odds, I choose to believe and take God at His Word...and His Word is LIFE to me. Furthermore, I fully expect Him to fulfill it and make it come to pass in Jesus' name.

~ Romans 4:17-18

I abide under the shadow of the Almighty and the protection of Psalm 91 promises, for I trust in the Lord as my refuge and fortress. He delivers me and shields me from all harm. No matter what happens around me, evil will not touch or affect me or my household. Because of His love, I am secure and will experience the fullness of His salvation.

~ Psalm 91

---

Because I believe that ALL things are possible with my God, I have the authority to say to this seemingly 'impossible' situation, this mountain, this giant that I face *(name it)*—

_____
_____
_____
_____
_____

to be removed NOW in the mighty name of Jesus!

~ Mark 9:23, 11:23

Lord, according to Isaiah 43:26, I put You in remembrance of all these promises based on what You have said in Your Word. Plus, I remind you of

_____
_____
_____
_____
_____
_____
_____
_____
_____
_____
_____
_____
_____
_____
_____
_____
_____
_____

*(Include any formal petitions you have made of the Lord, prophesies that line up with the Word, any judgments you have received in your favour from the Courts of Heaven, etc. See Chapter 5, point #6).*

Therefore, because You are true to Your Word, Your promises, and Your judgments, I have total and complete victory along with recompense and repayment for my losses in Jesus' precious and holy name. The time is NOW! So be it! AMEN!

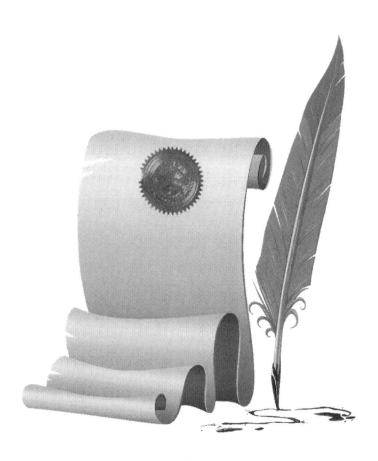

# Chapter Seven

## Take Your Stand!

In declaring and decreeing these promises, you are taking a decisive stand against the enemy. You are stating your case before the Lord using the evidence of the Word to back up your position. God's Word—which originates from the heart of the Father—contains all the promises and provision we all need to BE, to HAVE, and to DO according to our calling as believers and heirs with Christ. THIS IS, as part of our godly mandate, what it means to release and establish on earth what has already been determined in Heaven by our gracious and loving Father.

God created us to be more than conquerors in all things.[12] His design is and always has been for us to be victorious. In speaking out declarations and decrees, we ACT on the authority of His Word to take our stand and conquer the enemy.

---

[12] See Romans 8:37

The action of declaring and decreeing cooperates with faith so that we can receive what has been promised. It is a *powerful strategy* from the Lord for fighting our battles in the spiritual realm *first* in order to see results manifest in the physical realm. In all reality, it is GOD who is the One—through what is proclaimed in faith based on the Word—who is actually fighting the battle for us. The Word IS God![13]

NOW, it is TIME to take your stand! Speak out these decrees of victory in faith and confidence! I also encourage you to take the time to search the Scriptures for other promises of victory so that you may write out your own declarations to add to what has been included in this book.

---

[13] See John 1:1

# My Decrees

# About the Author

**Cheryl Regier** is a #1 best-selling author, a dedicated editor, an entrepreneur, mentor, trainer, and speaker.

She is the founder and president of Zachariah House Inc.—a business ministry of helps and services—which provides *Editing for Impact* and *Inside Out Health*. She is particularly passionate about partnering with authors to prepare their messages for the masses and has been the editor for a number of best-selling publications. Her invaluable reference guide, *Now What? A Guide Through the Editing Process*, is assisting authors further by serving as a checklist for preparing their work for the next step and helping them to successfully navigate the editing process with ease and understanding.

Her testimony is that the Lord is beyond faithful! In all the circumstances of her life, He has shown Himself to be trustworthy time and time again. Throughout it all, she has been trained and equipped for the specific call on her life, positioned by His grace to do the work of the Kingdom. Learning to live from a place of identity first—who God says she is—in order to have what she needs to do what God has called her to do (the "Be-Have-Do" model) has been an ongoing lesson in yielding to and partnering with the Holy Spirit. For all that the Lord has done along with the favour He has bestowed, she is and always will be eternally grateful.

Cheryl has been married to her wonderful husband, Brad, for over 27 years. They have been blessed with six amazing sons and one beautiful daughter-in-love. She currently resides in, Alberta, Canada.

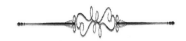

**Cheryl Regier**, a #1 best-selling author as well as a dedicated and passionate editor, is committed to delivering high-quality editing services through *Editing for Impact*, operating as part of Zachariah House Inc.

She provides editing for books—specializing in non-fiction, faith-based books—as well as workbooks, articles, brochures, promotional materials, websites, and more.

Her best-selling reference book, *Now What? A Guide Through the Editing Process*, helps authors prepare their writing for the next step and assists them in navigating the editing process with greater ease, saving them time, frustration, and money.

Approaching every manuscript or project in her docket from two main perspectives—one, of addressing the mechanics and structure of the work, and two, looking at it through the eyes of a reader and the big picture—her services result in an excellent finished product.

***Cheryl works diligently to enhance each author's message and voice for the greatest impact!***

*Editing for Impact* is a Division of Zachariah House Inc.
www.Zachariah-House.com
zachariahhouseofhelps@gmail.com

# To WRITE at the HIGHEST LEVEL,
you must be healthy from the inside out!

## What are you doing to INVEST in your health and wellness?

Address the B.I.G. three
—Blood sugars, Inflammation, Gut health—
and SEE and FEEL the difference in
ENERGY and FOCUS!
Set yourself up right to write!

### CHERYL REGIER

Inside Out Health Facilitator and Plexus Ambassador
www.plexusworldwide.ca/cherylregier

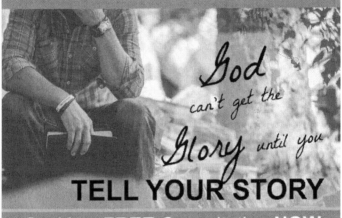

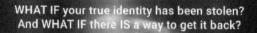

Manufactured by Amazon.ca
Bolton, ON

16288396R00031